Foundations of Democracy

Political Participation and Voting Rights

FOUNDATIONS OF DEMOCRACY

Citizenship and Immigration
Corruption and Transparency
Employment and Workers' Rights
Gender Equality and Identity Rights
Justice, Policing, and the Rule of Law
Political Participation and Voting Rights
Religious, Cultural, and Minority Rights
Speech, Media, and Protest

FOUNDATIONS OF DEMOCRACY

POLITICAL PARTICIPATION AND VOTING RIGHTS

Author and Series Advisor
Tom Lansford
Professor of Political Science
University of Southern Mississippi, Gulf Coast

MASON CREST

Mason Crest
450 Parkway Drive, Suite D
Broomall, PA 19008
www.masoncrest.com

© 2017 by Mason Crest, an imprint of National Highlights, Inc. All rights reserved. No part of this publication may be reproduced or transmitted in any form or by any means, electronic or mechanical, including photocopying, recording, taping, or any information storage and retrieval system, without permission from the publisher.

MTM Publishing, Inc.
435 West 23rd Street, #8C
New York, NY 10011
www.mtmpublishing.com

President: Valerie Tomaselli
Vice President, Book Development: Hilary Poole
Designer: Annemarie Redmond
Copyeditor: Peter Jaskowiak
Editorial Assistant: Andrea St. Aubin

Series ISBN: 978-1-4222-3625-3
Hardback ISBN: 978-1-4222-3631-4
E-Book ISBN: 978-1-4222-8275-5

Library of Congress Cataloging-in-Publication Data
Names: Lansford, Tom, author.
Title: Political participation and voting rights / by Tom Lansford.
Description: Broomall, PA: Mason Crest, 2017. | Series: Foundations of democracy | Includes index.
Identifiers: LCCN 2016004312| ISBN 9781422236314 (hardback) | ISBN 9781422236253 (series) | ISBN 9781422282755 (ebook)
Subjects: LCSH: Political participation—United States—Juvenile literature. | Suffrage—United States—Juvenile literature. | Voting—United States—Juvenile literature.
Classification: LCC JK1764 .L355 2017 | DDC 324.60973—dc23
LC record available at http://lccn.loc.gov/2016004312

Printed and bound in the United States of America.

First printing
9 8 7 6 5 4 3 2 1

TABLE OF CONTENTS

Series Introduction.. 7
Chapter One: Political Participation................................ 9
Chapter Two: Challenges to Political Participation 19
Chapter Three: Elections... 29
Chapter Four: Voting Rights... 39
Chapter Five: Challenges to Voting Rights....................... 48
Further Reading... 57
Series Glossary.. 58
Index.. 60
About the Author... 64
Photo Credits.. 64

Key Icons to Look for:

Words to Understand: These words with their easy-to-understand definitions will increase the reader's understanding of the text, while building vocabulary skills.

Sidebars: This boxed material within the main text allows readers to build knowledge, gain insights, explore possibilities, and broaden their perspectives by weaving together additional information to provide realistic and holistic perspectives.

Research Projects: Readers are pointed toward areas of further inquiry connected to each chapter. Suggestions are provided for projects that encourage deeper research and analysis.

Text-Dependent Questions: These questions send the reader back to the text for more careful attention to the evidence presented there.

Series Glossary of Key Terms: This back-of-the-book glossary contains terminology used throughout the series. Words found here increase the reader's ability to read and comprehend higher-level books and articles in this field.

Iraqi women at a political rally in 2010, in advance of the country's parliamentary elections.

SERIES INTRODUCTION

Democracy is a form of government in which the people hold all or most of the political power. In democracies, government officials are expected to take actions and implement policies that reflect the will of the majority of the citizenry. In other political systems, the rulers generally rule for their own benefit, or at least they usually put their own interests first. This results in deep differences between the rulers and the average citizen. In undemocratic states, elites enjoy far more privileges and advantages than the average citizen. Indeed, autocratic governments are often created to exploit the average citizen.

Elections allow citizens to choose representatives to make choices for them, and under some circumstances to decide major issues themselves. Yet democracy is much more than campaigns and elections. Many nations conduct elections but are not democratic. True democracy is dependent on a range of freedoms for its citizenry, and it simultaneously exists to protect and enhance those freedoms. At its best, democracy ensures that elites, average citizens, and even groups on the margins of society all have the same rights, privileges, and opportunities. The components of democracy have changed over time as individuals and groups have struggled to expand equality. In doing so, the very notion of what makes up a democracy has evolved. The volumes in this series examine the core freedoms that form the foundation of modern democracy.

Citizenship and Immigration explores what it means to be a citizen in a democracy. The principles of democracy are based on equality, liberty, and government by the consent of the people. Equality means that all citizens have the same rights and responsibilities. Democracies have struggled to integrate all groups and ensure full equality. Citizenship in a democracy is the formal recognition that a person is a member of the country's political community. Modern democracies have faced profound debates over immigration, especially how many people to admit to the country and what rights to confer on immigrants who are not citizens.

Challenges have also emerged within democracies over how to ensure disadvantaged groups enjoy full equality with the majority, or traditionally dominant, populations. While outdated legal or political barriers have been mostly removed, democracies still struggle to overcome cultural or economic impediments to equality. *Gender Equality and Identity Rights* analyzes why gender equality has proven especially challenging, requiring political, economic, and cultural reforms. Concurrently, *Religious, Cultural, and Minority Rights* surveys the efforts that democracies have undertaken to integrate disadvantaged groups into the political, economic, and social mainstream.

A free and unfettered media provides an important check on government power and ensures an informed citizenry. The importance of free expression and a free press are detailed in *Speech, Media, and Protest*, while *Employment and Workers' Rights* provides readers with an overview of the importance of economic liberty and the ways in which employment and workers' rights reinforce equality by guaranteeing opportunity.

The maintenance of both liberty and equality requires a legal system in which the police are constrained by the rule of law. This means that security officials understand and respect the rights of individuals and groups and use their power in a manner that benefits communities, not represses them. While this is the ideal, legal systems continue to struggle to achieve equality, especially among disadvantaged groups. These topics form the core of *Justice, Policing, and the Rule of Law*.

Corruption and Transparency examines the greatest danger to democracy: corruption. Corruption can undermine people's faith in government and erode equality. Transparency, or open government, provides the best means to prevent corruption by ensuring that the decisions and actions of officials are easily understood.

As discussed in *Political Participation and Voting Rights*, a government of the people requires its citizens to provide regular input on policies and decisions through consultations and voting. Despite the importance of voting, the history of democracies has been marked by the struggle to expand voting rights. Many groups, including women, only gained the right to vote in the last century, and continue to be underrepresented in political office.

Ultimately, all of the foundations of democracy are interrelated. Equality ensures liberty, while liberty helps maintain equality. Meanwhile, both are necessary for a government by consent to be effective and lasting. Within a democracy, all people must be treated equally and be able to enjoy the full range of liberties of the country, including rights such as free speech, religion, and voting.

—Tom Lansford

Chapter One

POLITICAL PARTICIPATION

Words to Understand

democracy: a political system in which citizens hold all or most political power.

interest group: an organization that is not a political party, but attempts to influence politics or the government.

national service: a period of voluntary or mandatory government service.

political participation: activities that influence, support, or just involve a nation's political culture and system.

terrorism: political violence designed to intimidate or coerce people and governments to accept the aims of the perpetrators.

tyranny: rule by a small group or single person.

D**emocracy** has become the most common form of government around the world. It provides the best way to prevent **tyranny**. Democracies rely on their citizens to play a role in decision-making processes, political activities, and the

POLITICAL PARTICIPATION AND VOTING RIGHTS

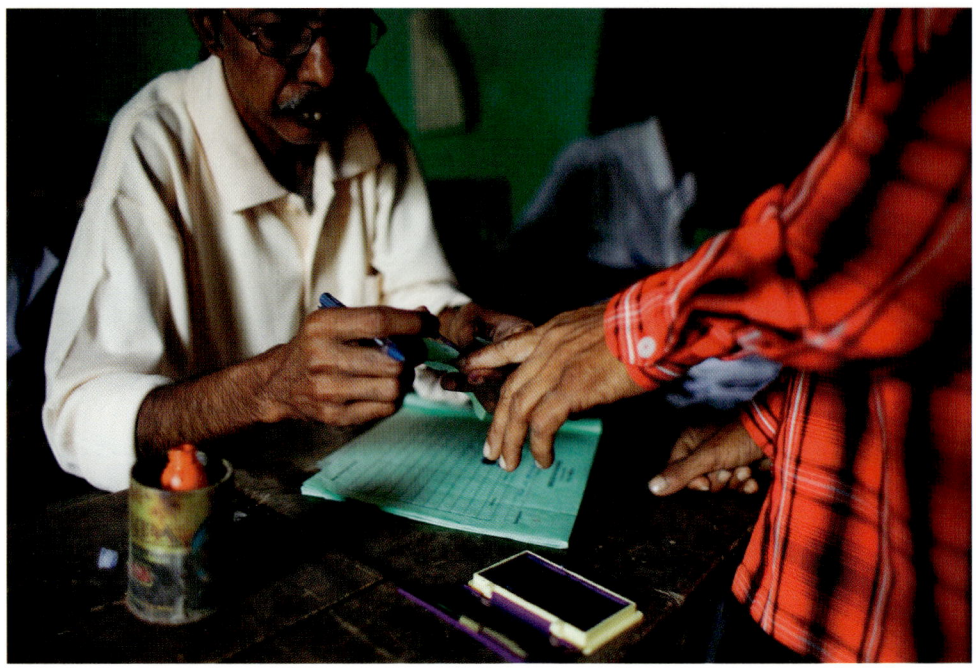

An Indian citizen has his finger stained with ink as he votes in his country's national elections in 2009.

governance of the country in a regulated manner. This gives citizens both a stake in the government and a means to voice their frustrations or concerns.

Democratic governments share a range of characteristics. First, citizens control the political processes and shape policy through elections, public opinion, and **political participation**. Second, governments strive to promote equality among their citizens and prevent any one group from dominating other portions of the population. Third, democracies provide citizens with access to power through regular, fair elections.

Formal Political Participation

Political participation is one of the foundations of democracy. It's the main way through which citizens exercise control over their government or influence policy decisions. There

CHAPTER ONE: POLITICAL PARTICIPATION

are two broad categories of political participation, formal and informal. Formal forms of participation include those sponsored by government, while informal types are organized and led by people outside of the government.

Voting is the most important form of formal political participation. Governing a country is too complex for all citizens to cast votes on every single issue, so elections are held to choose people who will represent voters' interests and make decisions on their behalf. Elections are organized by governments to give people regular access to political power (some forms of elections are overseen by nongovernmental bodies, such as political parties). Voting rights and different types of elections are discussed in further detail in subsequent chapters.

Members of Malaysia's national service on standby during the 57th National Day Parade of Malaysia at Merdeka Square, Kuala Lumpur.

11

POLITICAL PARTICIPATION AND VOTING RIGHTS

 ## NATIONAL SERVICE IN THE PHILIPPINES

In the Philippines, male and female college students are required to perform national service through one of three programs. The Civic Welfare Training Service (CWTS) includes educational, environmental, and social activities that are designed to benefit communities. For instance, students might be trained as teachers or social workers. The Literacy Training Service (LTS) specifically focuses on teaching literacy or mathematical proficiency to younger children or youths that have dropped out of school. Participants in either of these programs have to commit to two semesters of training and service, for which they receive college credit. The third program is the Reserve Officers' Training Corps (ROTC), which trains students to become officers in the military. Students in ROTC have to commit to four semesters of service. Between 2002 and 2012, 8.61 million students went through the CWTS program, 538,700 through LTS, and 1.44 million through ROTC.

Other formal forms of participation include various types of government service. For instance, a citizen might seek political office as an elected official. Citizens may serve in the military (in some countries, such as Canada or the United States, military service is voluntary, in other countries, such as Norway or Israel, it is required). An alternative to military service is **national service**, which may include teaching or even service as an emergency responder. Citizens may also be required to serve on a jury, as is the case in many nations, including Australia, the United Kingdom, and the United States.

Informal Political Participation

Informal political participation may be done on an individual level or as part of a group. For instance, a person might write a letter or an e-mail to a government official in order

12

CHAPTER ONE: POLITICAL PARTICIPATION

A volunteer outside a polling station in Montego Bay, Jamaica, during a national election in December 2011.

POLITICAL PARTICIPATION AND VOTING RIGHTS

to show support or opposition for a policy. Individuals might blog or use other forms of social media to comment on political developments.

Other forms of informal participation often revolve around political campaigns. Citizens might donate money to a candidate or a campaign to change public policy. They may also volunteer time for these efforts. Citizens can also volunteer to work at polls during elections or register people to vote. Sometimes such participation may take the form of membership in a political party or an **interest group**. It could also be as simple as donating money to a campaign, political party, or interest group.

Demonstrations and protests are among the most visible methods of informal participation. These manifestations of public opinion may range from a few people to hundreds of thousands gathered together. Protests may disrupt traffic and commerce. The majority of protests are peaceful, but they can turn violent, leading to damage to property and scuffles between demonstrators and security officials. During protests on November 25, 2014, following the shooting of Michael Brown in Ferguson, Missouri, more than 25 businesses were burned down, along with more than a dozen cars (including two police cars), and 80 people were arrested. Demonstrations can be a powerful political tool for people to voice their dissatisfaction with their government, however. Protests in January 2009 over the Icelandic government's management of the country's economic crisis led the prime minister to resign and schedule new elections.

Protests against governments or government actions can take many forms besides street demonstrations. For instance, people may occupy a building or site. Environmental protestors have chained themselves to trees to prevent them being cut down for timber or commercial development. Protests may also be expressed through violence, including armed rebellions or **terrorism**.

POLITICAL CONSULTATIONS

Governments often utilize a variety of different forms of political consultations with their citizens. These meetings provide an opportunity for officials to explain policy or seek

CHAPTER ONE: POLITICAL PARTICIPATION

THE OCCUPY MOVEMENT

In September 2011, demonstrators began a protest in New York they called Occupy Wall Street. The aim of the protestors was to highlight the inequalities in income and wealth around the world, and to demand government action to promote social and financial equality. Demonstrators decried the growth in wealth by the top 1 percent of the population, and dubbed themselves the "99 percent." Protests soon spread to other cities in the United States and around the world. By the following year, Occupy protests had taken place in more than 80 countries. However, governments also began to dismantle the Occupy camps, and the protests simmered out by the end of 2012. The movement did help focus attention on income inequality, and it energized young activists around the world.

Protesters at the Occupy Toronto protest in St. James Park.

POLITICAL PARTICIPATION AND VOTING RIGHTS

feedback from citizens on various issues. In many countries, it is common for citizens to be invited to local council meetings, where they are given time to comment on issues or express concerns about policies. Countries such as Norway or Canada require their municipal council meetings to be open to the public, with some exceptions for issues such as personnel matters.

Another form of political consultation involves listening sessions for elected officials to hear the opinions of their constituency. These sessions may range from very small, select groups to large gatherings. Sometimes officials will gather people to represent different constituencies, often seeking to include people from different races, religions, ethnicities, and genders. These folks are arranged into small gatherings known as "focus groups" and asked very specific questions on policies or issues.

A town hall meeting gets heated in Lebanon, Pennsylvania.

CHAPTER ONE: POLITICAL PARTICIPATION

 ## POLITICAL PARTICIPATION AND SOCIAL MEDIA

The rise of social media has dramatically expanded the ways in which citizens may engage in political participation. Platforms such as Facebook, Twitter, and even YouTube, provide politicians and political parties new ways to communicate with supporters, and citizens have new ways to exchange their thoughts, opinions, and plans. Social media delivers almost instantaneous news and responses, and therefore has a much more immediate feeling than traditional media.

One of the most significant means in which social media has impacted political participation has been through organizing protests and demonstrations. Organizers send out information on the time and place of a demonstration, and they can use social media to request various forms of support, including financial or material help. In India in 2011, social media played a key role in galvanizing more than 65,000 protesters in anticorruption demonstrations.

Larger sessions may be organized around a single issue or broad subjects, and they may include a single political figure or a group of officials. In the United States, the informal style of many of these gatherings is modeled on the New England town hall meeting, which allowed members of the community to come together to discuss and debate issues. The term "town hall meeting" has come to be synonymous with these types of sessions. The popularity of this format led to its incorporation in U.S. presidential debates in recent years. Candidates faced questions from the audience instead of professional journalists or other debate moderators.

At their most powerful and influential, political consultations may be called to deal with major issues. For instance, a nation may convene a constitutional convention to rewrite its basic laws or reform its government. These conventions often include both politicians and representatives of different civic, cultural, economic, or religious groups. In 1989, Scotland created a constitutional convention that included members of

POLITICAL PARTICIPATION AND VOTING RIGHTS

political parties, trade unions, business groups, churches, and so forth. The convention recommended a number of steps that led to greater political power for Scotland as part of the United Kingdom, including the establishment of a separate Scottish Parliament in 1999.

Text-Dependent Questions

1. What characteristics are shared by democratic governments?
2. What is the most important form of political participation, and why?
3. What are some of the different forms of informal political participation?

Research Projects

1. Research the history of military service in your country. Is service voluntary or compulsory? Write a brief report that highlights the advantages and disadvantages of conscription, and list those in an accompanying chart.
2. Research town hall meetings. Does your community use this form of political consultation? Write a report that explains how this type of political participation can make government more efficient.

Chapter Two

CHALLENGES TO POLITICAL PARTICIPATION

Words to Understand

neo-Nazi: an organization or political grouping that advocates the extremist policies and principles of the Nazi Party that ruled Germany from 1933 to 1945.

partisanship: a strong bias or prejudice toward one set of beliefs that often results in an unwillingness to compromise or accept alternative points of view.

political apathy: a lack of enthusiasm or interest in government or politics.

socioeconomic status: the position of a person within society, based on the combination of their income, wealth, education, family background, and social standing.

POLITICAL PARTICIPATION AND VOTING RIGHTS

Although democracies need political participation to function, there are a surprising variety of hurdles that citizens often have to navigate in order to be a part of the political process. In some cases, these obstacles may be based on race or **socioeconomic status**. In other instances, governments may restrict political participation in an effort to promote security or peace, especially during periods of conflict. For instance, governments may limit protests or demonstrations if officials fear violence or looting.

Outside the Russian embassy in London, protesters object to Russia's banning of Moscow Gay Pride gatherings.

CHAPTER TWO: CHALLENGES TO POLITICAL PARTICIPATION

Formal Challenges to Political Participation

Most democracies recognize that the right to assemble or protest is a fundamental human right. For instance, Article 11 of the European Convention on Human Rights declares people have the right to peacefully assemble. The First Amendment of the U.S. Constitution also guarantees that right. However, even with these protections, as mentioned above, governments do have the authority to ban protests. Police may control the route of a protest march, the location of a demonstration, or even the size of an assembly. These limitations are officially designed to maintain public order and minimize disruptions to those not involved in the protest. However, there are also occasions when authorities use these restrictions to suppress protests or demonstrations.

In the United Kingdom, local police officials have the right to ban all protests in a given area for up to three months if they assess that they would be unable to maintain public order during an event. These "banning orders" are usually issued after episodes of widespread violence, and they typically must be approved by a judge. In addition, most countries in Western Europe allow security officials to prohibit demonstrations that advocate violence or incite ethnic or religious hatred.

Authorities may also limit people's ability to express their opinions in political consultations. Some restrictions may be as simple and reasonable as limiting the amount of time people have to speak during public meetings. In other cases, meetings may be closed to the public. In the United States, for instance, local governments typically have the power to bar the public from what are known as "executive sessions." These meetings often revolve around personnel issues, such as the hiring or dismissal of a public official, negotiations over purchasing or contracts, or matters under litigation.

Governments may also ban certain political organizations. Typically these prohibitions are because the groups advocate violence or hatred toward one group or race or are extremist groups. For instance, West Germany banned the Socialist Reich Party (a **neo-Nazi** group) in 1952, and the Communist Party of Germany was banned

POLITICAL PARTICIPATION AND VOTING RIGHTS

A mural in London commemorates the Battle of Cable Street in 1936, in which police in Manchester clashed with members of the British Union of Fascists. The party was subsequently banned by the British government.

CHAPTER TWO: CHALLENGES TO POLITICAL PARTICIPATION

THE NATIONAL DEMOCRATIC PARTY OF GERMANY

In 1964, the National Democratic Party of Germany (Nationaldemokratische Partei Deutschlands, or NPD) was formed in Germany as a neo-Nazi grouping. The party is anti-Semitic and has been critical of other ethnic and religious minorities in Germany, including immigrants. It has also called for the elimination of democracy. In 2001 the government attempted to ban the NPD, arguing that the party posed a threat to democracy because it called for the abolishment of Germany's constitution. Germany's high court rejected the effort, however, declaring that the party did not pose an "immediate threat" to democracy. Many opponents of the party nonetheless argued that it would be wrong to ban the party unless it was engaged in illegal activity. Otherwise, although its views are not popular and are condemned by mainstream parties, some have argued that democracies must tolerate unpleasant viewpoints. The government launched a new and ongoing bid to ban the NPD in 2013, but as of October 2015, no decision had been reached.

in 1956. In addition, groups or parties that advocate the overthrow of the existing government are often outlawed, especially if they call for the use of violence against the regime.

INFORMAL CHALLENGES TO POLITICAL PARTICIPATION

Informal challenges to political participation are often the result of socioeconomic inequalities. For instance, in many democracies, women are underrepresented in elected offices. In 2015, women comprised just 29.4 percent of the members of the British Parliament, 26.2 percent of the French National Assembly, and 19.4 percent

POLITICAL PARTICIPATION AND VOTING RIGHTS

France has laws that enforce gender parity in political office, but they are not uncontroversial. Center-right politician Michèle Alliot-Marie has described parity laws as "an insult to women."

CHAPTER TWO: CHALLENGES TO POLITICAL PARTICIPATION

 WOMEN IN LEGISLATURES

Women remain underrepresented in elected office in most countries. There are some exceptions, however. For instance, as of 2015, women comprise 63.8 percent of the members of Rwanda's lower house of Parliament (51 of 80 seats), and 38.5 percent of the upper house (10 of 26 seats). Women made such strides partly as the result of a national law that requires that the candidates from political parties be at least 30 percent female. Other countries have adopted similar legislation, known as gender quotas, to force parties to seek and run more women for office. A growing number of political parties have enacted voluntary gender quotas, including the Australian Labour Party (40 percent), the French Socialist Party (50 percent), and the Italian Democratic Party (50 percent).

of the U.S. House of Representatives. Among advanced democracies, Sweden has the highest percentage of women legislators, with 43.6 percent. Women also often vote in lower numbers, especially younger women. In the United Kingdom in 2010, only 39 percent of women between the ages of 18 and 24 voted, compared with 50 percent of men in the same age group. Ethnic and racial minorities also typically have lower rates of participation, as well as lower rates of representation in government.

The underrepresentation of women and minority groups in politics is certainly one factor in lower voter turnout among these populations. Without role models or figures with which individuals can identify, people are less likely to be politically active or run for office. Another factor may be outdated and discriminatory cultural ideas that discourage participation by women and disadvantaged groups. A person's parents are usually the most important influence on their political beliefs. Consequently, groups with little history of political participation are in danger of perpetuating traditions of nonparticipation.

POLITICAL PARTICIPATION AND VOTING RIGHTS

Economic factors can also pay a significant role in reducing political participation. Less affluent members of society are less likely to contribute money to political parties or causes. Lower-income workers may also have less time to volunteer for political campaigns and be less willing to seek elected office.

APATHY

One of the greatest challenges to political participation is **political apathy**. Among the democracies of Western Europe and North America, there has been a general trend away from political participation, especially among younger citizens. The decline in participation has been manifested in a variety of ways, including lower voter turnout, reductions in political party membership, and drops in attendance at political consultations. In the United Kingdom, voter turnout has been significantly lower in national elections in the 21st century than it was in the 20th century, when it averaged more than 70 percent (turnout was 59 percent in 2001, 61 percent in 2005, 65 percent in 2010, and 66.1 percent in 2015). In 2010 the journal *The Economist* found that political party membership in 13 European democracies declined by 40 percent during a 20-year period beginning in the late 1970s. Meanwhile, politicians throughout Western Europe and North America have found reduced audiences at public meetings and events.

Why has political apathy increased? There are a number of possible factors. First, people may believe that the government and the existing political parties do not adequately represent their values or interests. Second, people lose faith in the government's ability to accomplish goals or solve problems. This is more prevalent during periods of extreme **political partisanship**, when citizen often perceive that officials are more interested in gains for their party or group, instead of the greater good of the country. Third, there is a sense that an individual cannot influence the political process. People feel that their "vote does not count," or that their "voice" is not heard. Fourth, the rise of social media has made it easier for people to communicate political views without formal interaction. People no longer need to go to meetings to find

CHAPTER TWO: CHALLENGES TO POLITICAL PARTICIPATION

Activists for marijuana legalization in Washington State worked to get more young voters registered at events like Seattle Hempfest.

POLITICAL PARTICIPATION AND VOTING RIGHTS

information on policies or to express views. While this has encouraged some forms of informal political participation, it has also made people less likely to attend town hall meetings, for instance.

Text-Dependent Questions

1. What are the main formal challenges to political participation?
2. How does the underrepresentation of some groups impact political participation?
3. Why has political apathy increased in recent years?

Research Projects

1. Research the concept of freedom of expression. Should groups or political parties that espouse racial or ethnic hatred be banned? Write an editorial defending your view.
2. Research political partisanship. Write an essay on how partisanship harms political participation and what steps may be taken to overcome these types of political divisions.

Chapter Three

ELECTIONS

Words to Understand

bicameral: a legislature with two chambers, usually with some difference in power and authority.

canton: an administrative subdivision of a country; the term is most associated with Switzerland, but other countries use it, including Ecuador, France, and Luxembourg.

referendum: a vote in which all citizens have the opportunity to express their preference, usually on a single issue.

sovereignty: supreme authority over people and geographic space. National governments have sovereignty over their citizens and territory.

tyranny of the majority: in democracies, when the majority uses its political, economic, or social power to implement policies that reflect its interests without regard for the well-being or needs of minorities or disadvantaged groups.

POLITICAL PARTICIPATION AND VOTING RIGHTS

Pro-independence voters in Glasgow on the day of the national referendum. Ultimately, Scotland voted to remain part of the United Kingdom.

CHAPTER THREE: ELECTIONS

As noted in chapter one, voting is the most meaningful and influential form of political participation for most citizens. Elections provide a regular means for citizens to express their approval, disapproval, and even anger toward governments and their policies. Free, fair, and open elections are one of the defining characteristics of democracies.

There are a wide variety of elections. People are asked to vote on candidates for various political offices and on diverse issues such as tax increases or even independence from existing political structures. The organization and conduct of elections plays a significant role in determining the level of participation in the balloting and the legitimacy of the vote.

Direct Democracy and Elections

There are two basic types of democracy: direct and representative. These distinct forms determine the type of polling used during elections. *Direct democracy* is when people themselves make decisions on issues. Typically, this involves all eligible citizens being given an opportunity to express their preference through a vote. Instead of the government making a decision on an issue, it is left in the hands of the people. For instance, on September 18, 2014, the people of Scotland voted in a **referendum** on whether to become independent of the United Kingdom. The vote was 55.3 percent against independence and 44.7 percent in favor. There was a record voter turnout of 84.6 percent, demonstrating how some referendums may boost voter participation.

Many countries use this type of ballot initiative to allow citizens to decide major issues. The referendum may be put before voters by the government. In some nations, certain issues are required to be approved by referendum. Examples of these types of matters would be changes to the constitution or other issues that impact state **sovereignty**. For instance, Croatia held a referendum on January 22, 2012, on whether or not to join the European Union (66.7 percent of the population voted yes, and 33.3 percent voted no). In other cases, governments are unable or unwilling to decide an issue and pass it on to voters.

POLITICAL PARTICIPATION AND VOTING RIGHTS

 ## REFERENDUMS AND VOTER TURNOUT

Depending on the issue, a referendum may dramatically increase voter turnout. If a popular or contentious issue is part of a referendum, more citizens are likely to vote. This encourages political parties to add referendums to general elections in order to get more of their supporters to the polls. In Switzerland, for example, the anti-immigrant Swiss People's Party called for a referendum to restrict the nation's asylum policy prior to the 1999 elections. The referendum passed with 70.6 percent of the vote. Meanwhile, the party increased its vote share in the general election from 14.9 percent in the 1995 balloting to 22.5 percent in 1999, and it went from 29 seats in the Federal Assembly to 44.

Not all referenda receive a high turn out. Armenia held a constitutional referendum in November 2015, and only about 50 percent of the population voted. This antigovernment poster reads, "No to the criminal regime's new constitution."

CHAPTER THREE: ELECTIONS

Some countries, including Italy, New Zealand, and Switzerland, allow citizens to initiate a referendum at the national level. Other countries, including the United States, permit ballot initiatives at the state or local level. Citizens must usually acquire a minimum number of signatures of registered voters in support of adding the measure to the ballot. For instance, in Colorado in 2012, supporters of legalizing the personal use of marijuana had to get 85,853 signatures. The measure was then put before voters on November 6, 2012, when it was approved, 55.3 percent to 44.7 percent, thus legalizing the drug in the state.

Another electoral form of direct democracy is the recall. Recalls allow citizens to vote an elected official out of office. Like referendums, a recall requires a percentage of the electorate to petition for a vote to remove an official from office. For instance, in Switzerland, applicants must gather signatures from between 2 and 7 percent of the population, depending on the **canton**, to force a recall. In the United States, 20 states and the District of Columbia allow recalls in some form at the state level, while 29 states allow recalls for local officials.

REPRESENTATIVE DEMOCRACY AND ELECTIONS

The second type of democracy is *representative democracy*. In these systems, citizens elect representatives, who then make choices on their behalf. Regular elections provide citizens the ability to provide input on the performance of those who represent them, and to replace those representatives if necessary. If representatives do not support policies that are endorsed by their constituents, they are not likely to be re-elected.

Representatives serve in a legislative body, whether it is a local council, a state or regional legislature, or a national parliament or congress. Legislative bodies may have one chamber, or they may be **bicameral**. The terms of these elected officials are determined by their nation's constitution, and typically range from two to five years, when a new election occurs.

POLITICAL PARTICIPATION AND VOTING RIGHTS

The House of Representatives in Nigeria, one half of the country's bicameral legislature, which was modeled on the U.S. Congress.

Representative democracy is not only the most common form of democracy, but it is also the only system used at the national level in democratic countries around the world. In representative democracies, elected officials may concentrate their time and energy on studying issues and policies to a degree that most average citizens cannot match. In addition, elected officials provide continuity in policy whereas public opinion might change rapidly on issues. Elected representatives may also make difficult choices that the public would avoid. For instance, most people are reluctant to raise taxes, even when there is a significant need. Finally, since representatives are only elected every few years, elections are less frequent and less likely to lead to voter apathy.

CHAPTER THREE: ELECTIONS

THE PROBLEMS OF DIRECT AND REPRESENTATIVE DEMOCRACY

While direct democracy allows the greatest level of citizen control over policy matters, it has a number of problems. First, it can be difficult to compromise on sensitive or divisive issues. The result is what is often described as the **tyranny of the majority**, where the majority forces its will upon minority groups. This reflects the problem that public opinion is not always correct on an issue. Instead, it often evolves over time. At one time in the United States, for example, the majority of whites opposed full political rights for African Americans and other minorities. Second, not all citizens will appropriately study issues to the point where they can make informed choices. Third, direct democracy can lead to dramatic changes in policy, making it difficult for government officials to plan

HOW TO DETERMINE THE WINNER

There are a number of methods used to determine the winner in elections. In a winner-take-all system, also known as a first-past-the-post system, the candidate with the most votes is the winner. For instance, if there were three candidates running for office, with vote totals of 50 percent, 30 percent, and 20 percent, the candidate with 50 percent would win, even though 50 percent of the population voted against him or her.

In a proportional system, seats are allocated based on the percentage of votes received by political parties. Let us assume there were 10 seats up for election, and the candidates represent three different political parties. One party received 50 percent of the vote, the next got 30 percent, and the third got 20 percent. The leading party would get 5 seats, the second party would receive 3, and the last party would get 2. Proponents of the proportional system argue that it makes it easier for smaller parties to get elected, and that it therefore increases voter turnout by offering citizens more choice.

and carry-out policy. Fourth, direct democracy may lead to lower rates of participation if citizens began to feel overwhelmed by the need to vote on every issue or policy faced by government.

ELECTORAL COLLEGES

In some electoral systems, voters do not directly choose candidates. Instead, their votes are used to determine electors who then cast the final ballots for the office. This system is known as an "electoral college." For instance, in France, the upper chamber of the national legislature, the Senate, is chosen by an electoral college comprising about 150,000 elected officials, ranging from mayors and city council members to regional officials.

In the United States, electors are chosen according to which candidate wins the popular vote in a given state. The number of electors is determined by the population of the state and corresponds with that state's congressional delegation. In the 2012 presidential election, California had 55 electoral votes, followed by Texas with 34, while Alaska, Montana, North Dakota, South Dakota, Vermont, and Wyoming each had 3. In the United States, to become president, a candidate must receive the majority of the 538 electoral votes (if no one wins a majority of electoral votes, the House of Representatives chooses the president).

Electoral colleges provide a means to allow local or regional governments input into the election of senior officials. However, they also lead people to feel disconnected from elections and to perceive that their vote "does not count." In 2000, for example, the Republican presidential candidate, George W. Bush, won the presidential election, although the Democrat candidate, Al Gore, received the majority of the popular vote, 50,999,897 to 50,456,002. Without the electoral college, Gore would have won the election. The 2000 election was the fourth time in U.S. history that the winner of the popular vote did not win the presidency.

CHAPTER THREE: ELECTIONS

In 2000 the U.S. presidential election hinged on just a few votes cast in Palm Beach County, Florida. One of the ballot boxes and voting stands used in that disputed election is now part of a museum in Tallahassee.

Representative democracy also has a number of potential flaws. Representatives may become detached or isolated from their constituencies and not vote to promote the people's interests (this is especially true in cases of political corruption). This may also reduce political participation, if citizens feel disconnected from their representatives. Voters may also be less inclined to study issues and instead simply defer to their elected representatives.

POLITICAL PARTICIPATION AND VOTING RIGHTS

The problems inherent in both direct and representative democracy can lead to lower political participation. Citizens may feel as if their vote or voice does not count and, therefore, decide not to go to the polls. Restrictions on voting rights can exacerbate this problem.

Text-Dependent Questions

1. Why do governments sometimes use referendums to decide issues?
2. Why is representative democracy more common than direct democracy?
3. What are the main drawbacks of both direct and representative democracy?

Research Projects

1. Research direct democracy. Write an essay arguing whether or not a country could be ruled through direct democracy. What would be the advantages or disadvantages of such a system at the national level?
2. Research the U.S. electoral college. Write a brief report on the system and include a chart that presents the instances when the electoral college vote differed from the popular vote.

Chapter Four

VOTING RIGHTS

Words to Understand

demagogue: a political figure who seeks power by appealing to the emotions, fears, and prejudices of people, usually promising results that cannot be delivered.

Jim Crow era: the period in U.S. history from the end of Reconstruction until 1965, during which states enacted various discriminatory laws that segregated African Americans and severely restricted the right to vote among African Americans in many parts of the country.

poll tax: a fee that has to be paid in order to vote.

suffrage: the right to vote.

youth rights movement: an international, grassroots movement that advocates for greater political, economic, and social rights for people under the age of 21.

As noted in a previous chapter, voting is one of the most important forms of political participation. Democracies depend on citizens to vote as a way to endorse a current government and current policies, or to provide legitimacy

POLITICAL PARTICIPATION AND VOTING RIGHTS

A pro-suffrage journal from 1918: the figure of national suffrage is the friend of the forces of democracy.

40

CHAPTER FOUR: VOTING RIGHTS

for a new government or new initiatives. Elections are consequently the most important political action in contemporary democracies.

Questions over who can vote have led to recurring disputes in democracies. Historically, many groups have been excluded from the franchise (the right to vote). The story of voting rights has been the struggle to expand the franchise to disadvantaged populations. For instance, among most early democracies, such as the United Kingdom or the United States, only about 10 percent of the population had **suffrage** in the late 1700s. Disadvantaged groups such as women, minorities, and the poor could not vote.

ROTTEN BOROUGHS AND POCKET BOROUGHS

Voting rights were restricted to a small number of landowners and elites in Great Britain and Ireland until the franchise was gradually expanded in the 1800s. Meanwhile, the boundaries of the voting districts, or boroughs, remained unchanged for centuries, even if the population in a borough had decreased. The result was that some boroughs had less than 100 voting citizens. These were known as "rotten boroughs." The most extreme included Old Sarum in Wiltshire, in southwest Britain, which had only seven people eligible to vote by the end of the 1700s. Nevertheless, it still elected 2 of the 406 members of Parliament.

Great Britain also had "pocket boroughs" where large landowners controlled the votes of their tenants. At the time, secret ballots were not used, so everyone knew how a person voted. Landowners would evict or otherwise punish tenants who did not vote to their liking. It was also common to pay or otherwise reward voters for their support. Most of the rotten boroughs were eliminated through reforms in 1832, while reforms to the boundaries of boroughs in 1867 and the introduction of the secret ballot in 1872 meant the end of pocket boroughs.

POLITICAL PARTICIPATION AND VOTING RIGHTS

The Struggle for Universal Suffrage

Today, one of the hallmarks of a democracy is universal suffrage, or voting rights for almost all citizens. Even as countries began to adopt democracy in the 1700s and 1800s, almost all of these governments limited the right to vote. At the time, many political, social, and economic leaders argued against expanding the franchise to all citizens. The poor and underclass were considered incapable of making rational decisions about candidates. Elites feared that commoners would be easily misled by **demagogues** who sought power for personal gain. Of course, elites also feared that commoners would seek to redistribute wealth or land, and therefore undermine the advantages of those with the most power and influence in society at the time.

In order to restrict suffrage, governments enacted property requirements for voters. For instance, in Delaware, before the American Revolution (1775–1783) a voter had to own a minimum of 50 acres of land, or have business or property worth £40 (about $144,250 in today's currency). Many nations retained property restrictions into the 1900s. The United Kingdom did not end all property requirements for suffrage until 1928.

Women were generally excluded from voting until the late 1800s. Iceland, Finland, Sweden, some localities and colonies of the United Kingdom, and some states of the United States, granted women the right to vote in local balloting in the mid-to-late 1800s. For instance, Wyoming gave women the right to vote in 1869, followed by Utah, a year later. New Zealand was the first country to grant the franchise to women, in 1893. Most other democracies extended full suffrage in the first half of the 1900s, including the United States in 1920, the United Kingdom in 1928, and France in 1945.

Ethnic and racial minorities were also often excluded from voting. In the United States, African American and other minority males were not granted the right to vote at the national level until the Fifteenth Amendment was ratified in 1870. Even following that measure, many states enacted a variety of laws during the **Jim Crow era** that effectively restricted voting until the Voting Rights Act of 1965 was passed.

CHAPTER FOUR: VOTING RIGHTS

A march from Selma to Montgomery, Alabama, on behalf of civil rights, in 1965.

There were also early religious restrictions on voting. For example, Catholics were not allowed to vote in the United Kingdom until 1829. Meanwhile, Catholics and other religious minorities, such as Jews and Quakers, could not vote in most of the British colonies in America until after the American Revolution.

The final widespread barrier to universal suffrage was age. Most countries set the minimum voting age as 21 through the 18th and 19th centuries. During the 20th century, most nations lowered the voting age to 18, including France and the United Kingdom in 1969, and the United States in 1971. The rationale for lowering the voting age was that in most countries people could marry, own property, and serve in the military at 18, and they therefore deserved to have a say in national debates on these types of issues. Some

POLITICAL PARTICIPATION AND VOTING RIGHTS

VOTING RESTRICTIONS AND INTIMIDATION DURING THE JIM CROW ERA

The Fifteenth Amendment to the U.S. Constitution (1870) prohibited states from restricting suffrage based on race or ethnicity. However, groups such as the Ku Klux Klan (KKK) launched campaigns to intimidate minority voters and whites that would not support candidates endorsed by the KKK. The actions of the KKK led the government to enact the Civil Rights Act of 1871 (also known as the Ku Klux Klan Act), which allowed the president to use military force against the Klan and expanded penalties for voter interference.

After the Reconstruction period (1865–1877), southern states, along with some others, such as Oklahoma and Maryland, began to enact measures that effectively served to disenfranchise African American voters without specifically mentioning race. For instance, states required literacy tests to determine the ability of potential voters to read and write, and therefore, supposedly understand issues and differentiate between candidates. In practice, the tests were extremely unfair and levied in such a way that biased officials could disqualify African Americans. The tests were used to disenfranchise African Americans, since white officials typically failed those attempting to pass the exam. Whites were often exempted from the literacy tests by the "grandfather clause," which mandated that a person whose grandfather was registered to vote before 1867 could skip the exams.

States also implemented **poll taxes** as a means of limiting voting rights. Southern states enacted poll taxes to limit African American suffrage, while other states, such as California, adopted the fees to restrict the likelihood that poor whites or immigrants would vote. Poll taxes were usually the equivalent of about $20 in today's currency. The poll tax was abolished by the Twenty-Fourth Amendment in 1964, while the 1965 Voting Rights Act forbade the use of literacy tests.

CHAPTER FOUR: VOTING RIGHTS

nations have even lower voting ages, including Argentina, Brazil, and Scotland, all with 16 as the minimum age for suffrage.

Contemporary Restrictions within Modern Democracies

With restrictions removed on the franchise for women, disadvantaged groups, and the less affluent, many democracies—such as Australia, France, and the United States—are said to have universal suffrage. However, a number of debates continue over voting rights. The issue of the voting age remains debated in many countries, especially in Western Europe, where the **youth rights movement** pushes for reductions in minimum age for the franchise to 16. Austria lowered its voting age to 16 in 2007, and there are continuing efforts to reduce the age for suffrage in other countries, including the United Kingdom.

Another issue of continuing debate is whether or not noncitizens should have voting rights. Universal suffrage means that all citizens, with some minor exceptions, have the right to vote. However, some democracies have begun to expand voting rights to even noncitizens who reside permanently in the country. For instance, 17 of the 29 countries of the European Union allow noncitizens to vote in local elections if they have lived in their host country for a specific period of time. Advocates for voting for noncitizens argue that residents live and work in the community, pay taxes, and use public services, and therefore deserve to be involved in the political process. Opponents assert that noncitizens do not have the same ties or loyalty to the country and should seek to gain citizenship if they want to vote.

Denmark, Estonia, Portugal, and Sweden have 3-year minimum requirements to vote in local balloting, while 5 years is required in Belgium, Luxembourg, and the Netherlands (other countries have periods ranging from 4 to 10 years). Some countries have reciprocity agreements whereby the citizens of one country are allowed to vote in another, provided that country grants the same rights to citizens of the first country.

POLITICAL PARTICIPATION AND VOTING RIGHTS

People voting in a school in Barcelona. Citizens of certain other countries are allowed to vote in Spanish elections, and vice versa, because of agreements worked out under the European Union.

Norway and Spain have such an arrangement, for example, so that Norwegian citizens may vote in Spain, and vice versa.

Some countries restrict the franchise of convicted criminals. Countries such as Austria, the United Kingdom, the United States, and Hungary do not allow convicts to vote while they are serving their sentences. However, other nations, including Canada, Finland, and Spain, allow criminals to vote even while they are in prison. Further complicating the issue is the practice in several nations to ban convicted criminals from voting even after they have left prison. Depending on the crime, judges may ban convicts from voting, even after they leave jail, in Bulgaria, France, and Malta, among other

CHAPTER FOUR: VOTING RIGHTS

countries. Nations such as Luxembourg, the Netherlands, and Slovakia impose short-term restrictions depending on the seriousness of the crime. In the United States, 48 states restrict the voting rights of people convicted of major crimes after they leave prison (Maine and Vermont do not).

TEXT-DEPENDENT QUESTIONS

1. Why did elites within society oppose universal suffrage in the 1700s and 1800s?
2. What are the arguments for and against allowing noncitizens to vote in local elections?
3. Why was the voting age lowered to 18 as part of the effort to expand the franchise?

RESEARCH PROJECTS

1. Research the voting age. Write an essay on what should be the minimum age to vote in national elections, and explain your reasoning.
2. Research voting restrictions on criminals. Write an essay on whether or not people serving time in prison should be allowed to vote.

Chapter Five

CHALLENGES TO VOTING RIGHTS

Words to Understand

absentee ballot: a ballot that is finalized and submitted before an election by a voter who is physically unable to appear at a polling place.
emerging democracies: countries that are transitioning to democracy from authoritarian rule.
malware: malicious software programs that damage or manipulate electronic devices such as computers, tablets, and smartphones.
military coup: the overthrow of an existing government by that nation's military, which typically then institutes a new regime or political system.

Although more and more democracies have enacted universal suffrage, there remain a variety of challenges to voting rights. Many barriers continue to exist that restrict access to polling places or that otherwise make it difficult for citizens to register to vote or cast ballots.

CHAPTER FIVE: CHALLENGES TO VOTING RIGHTS

In Istanbul, a giant election banner with a portrait of Turkish prime minister Ahmet Davutoğlu promises a "New Turkey."

POLITICAL PARTICIPATION AND VOTING RIGHTS

Not all countries, and indeed not even all democracies, have adopted universal suffrage. In Saudi Arabia, for instance, women are only allowed to vote in local elections (and they only gained that right in 2015). In other countries, such as Afghanistan, women have the right to vote, but they often face harassment and intimidation when they do so. Some countries with histories of **military coups** forbid voting by the military or police. Columbia, Egypt, and Turkey are examples of such states.

More common are informal or even illegal barriers to voting. In **emerging democracies**, the laws and protections that are needed to ensure voting rights are often weakly enforced. People may face unnecessary or even illegal hurdles when trying to vote. For instance, in South Africa's elections in 2014, election monitors and human rights observers found that some officials in the ruling African National Congress used threats of physical force or promises to end pensions or public assistance to coerce people into voting for their party. During Russia's 2012 presidential elections, there were reports that election observers were threatened or intimidated, often being forced to leave polling places, while voters who tried to file complaints over various issues faced physical violence.

CHALLENGES TO ACCESS

Even those countries with universal suffrage continue to face challenges in attempting to make sure that all eligible citizens can vote. Access to voting has emerged as the main challenge for contemporary voting rights within mature democracies. Central to this issue is the traditional form of elections whereby citizens go to a central location, a polling place, to cast ballots. Those who are disabled, temporarily incapacitated or sick, or who are travelling or working outside of the country cannot vote in the normal way. Consequently, democracies implemented new methods of voting to overcome issues of distance and access.

One of the earliest efforts at accommodation was the **absentee ballot**. These advanced ballots allowed voters who were unable to be present at a polling station

CHAPTER FIVE: CHALLENGES TO VOTING RIGHTS

VOTER IDENTIFICATION LAWS

There are intense debates in the United States over laws that require citizens to show identification (ID) in order to vote. These "voter ID laws" are decried by opponents, who view them as a means to suppress turnout in elections, since poor and disadvantaged voters are less likely to have government-issued ID. In addition, because of the history of discrimination in some states, demands for ID could be intimidating because of fears of reprisal. Opponents also point out that countries such as Australia, Denmark, and Great Britain do not require ID to vote.

Proponents of voter ID laws claim the measures reduce fraud. In many developed democracies, such as those in Canada, Western Europe, and India, voters are required to present ID. However, many of those countries already require citizens to have a national ID card. Countries such as India allow a person to use 1 of 15 different documents to vote, including income tax records or property deeds.

Voter ID materials from France.

POLITICAL PARTICIPATION AND VOTING RIGHTS

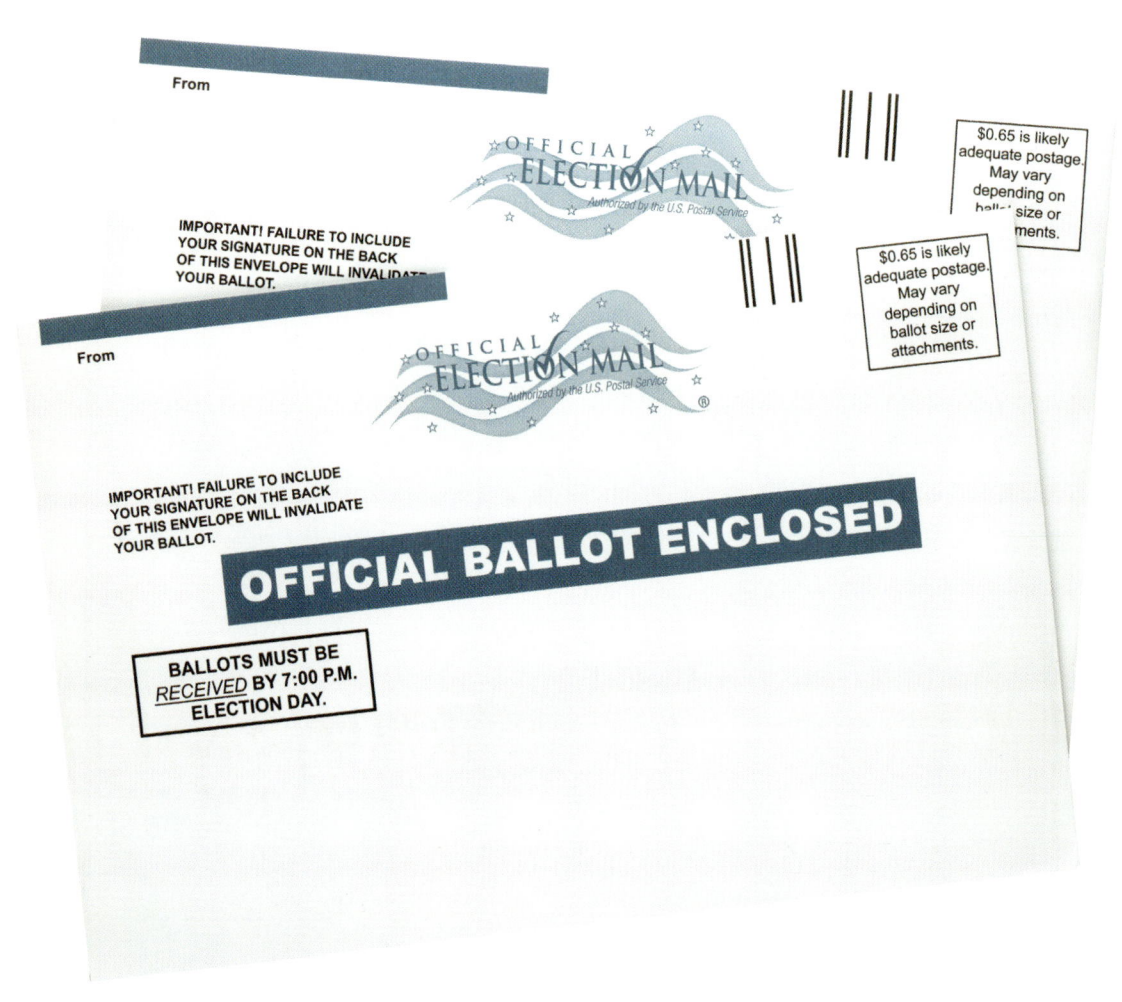

Sample mail-in ballots issued by the state of Colorado.

to vote by completing special paperwork and submitting their vote early, usually through the mail. In the United States, absentee ballots were first widely used during the Civil War (1861–1865) in an effort to make sure soldiers were able to vote in the 1864 national elections. The soldiers were given ballots, which they completed and then mailed to their home voting precinct.

    Absentee ballots are not a perfect solution for all occasions. People may be forced to travel or move unexpectedly, for example. Also, soldiers or workers in remote

CHAPTER FIVE: CHALLENGES TO VOTING RIGHTS

areas around the world may have difficulty getting or sending mail. Absentee ballots usually have deadlines for submission, creating questions over how to deal with ballots that are received after the deadline.

New Approaches to Voting and Voting Rights

In an effort to streamline the absentee ballot process and give greater access to the disabled or place-bound, an increasing number of communities have begun to utilize online voting. The small nation of Estonia allows citizens to vote in all elections online, through the use of national identity cards. In addition, more than 80 communities in Canada allow citizens to vote online in local balloting. In both Estonia and Canada,

---

I-VOTING AND ESTONIA

Estonia is a small country in the Baltic region, with a population of just 1.3 million. Its tech-savvy population was highly supportive of a pilot program in 2005 in which people were allowed to vote through the Internet (I-voting). Only about 1.9 percent of the population used I-voting, but the test was seen as a success, and the government decided to expand the program to include national elections over the next decade. By the 2015 national elections, 30.5 percent of voters cast their ballots over the Internet. Estonia also uses early voting (beginning six days before election day), but voters are allowed to change their vote as many times as they want until the final results are counted. To ensure security, voters use a national ID smart card that contains a variety of security protocols. Despite I-voting's success and popularity, IT experts continue to caution that it would be possible for hackers to infiltrate the system and manipulate the results through **malware**. As a result, many countries have been hesitant to use online voting.

voter participation rates increased substantially after online voting was introduced. However, critics of online voting underscore the potential for massive voter fraud. There is no secure way to ensure that someone voting from their home is not being threatened or intimidated. In addition, the possibility for electoral systems to be hacked remains a major threat. If a system were hacked, there would likely be no way to tell the "real" votes from fraudulent ones. The risks of fraud led the U.S. military to end an experimental online voting program, the Secure Electronic Registration and Voting Experiment (SERVE) in 2004, after only a year of trying the program.

A more simplistic approach has been to expand the time frame for voting. Instead of only allowing citizens to vote during specified hours on a single day, a growing number of countries and communities have expanded so-called early voting. This permits citizens to vote weeks in advance of an election. Countries such as Australia, Canada, Finland, and Thailand allow early voting. Thirty-three states in the United States also permit early voting.

APATHY

As with other forms of political participation, apathy is one of the most serious challenges to voting rights. In some countries, voters are automatically registered to vote using public records. This ensures almost total registration of potential voters. In other countries, the obligation to register to vote rests with the individual citizen. This results in lower voter registration rates and lower rates of participation.

In Canada, citizens are automatically registered to vote when they turn 18. In the United States, people must register themselves (although "motor-voter" laws allow citizens to register to vote when they acquire or renew their driver's license). When people move, they must update their voter registration. The result is that 93 percent of eligible Canadians were registered to vote in 2009, compared with just 68 percent of Americans. One solution being used in some U.S. states is same-day voter registration, which allows people to register and vote on the same day. Critics of same-day registration assert that

CHAPTER FIVE: CHALLENGES TO VOTING RIGHTS

Australian citizens voting in a parliamentary election in 2010.

POLITICAL PARTICIPATION AND VOTING RIGHTS

it increases the likelihood of fraud, since it is difficult to verify addresses and other information on the day of an election.

Compulsory voting is, of course, a more effective means to ensure voter participation. Countries which require all citizens to vote have higher turnout rates than those that do not. Twenty-two nations around the world, including Argentina, Belgium, Lebanon, and Singapore, require all citizens to vote. The punishment for failing to vote varies. In Australia, failure to vote results in a fine of $15 for the first offense, and $36 for subsequent offenses. In Greece, someone who fails to vote cannot get a new passport or driver's license until they cast a ballot in subsequent elections. Since voting is mandatory, many of these countries have taken greater steps to improve access for all citizens to vote.

The importance of voting cannot be overemphasized. Even with universal suffrage, challenges remain for voting rights. However, democratic nations continue to seek new policies or solutions that allow citizens to enjoy their full voting rights.

Text-Dependent Questions

1. What are some barriers to voting in countries with universal suffrage?
2. Why were absentee ballots initially used in the United States?
3. What are some of the potential problems with online voting?

Research Projects

1. Research online voting. Complete a brief report that discusses the topic and prepare a graph that outlines the benefits and potential drawbacks of online voting.
2. Research voter identification laws in the United States. Write a report that argues whether or not people should present IDs before they vote.

FURTHER READING

Books

Bynoe, Yvonne. *Stand and Deliver: Political Activism, Leadership and Hip Hop Culture.* Brooklyn, NY: Soft Skull Press, 2004.

Fisher, Dana. *Activism Inc.: How the Outsourcing of Grassroots Campaigns is Strangling Progressive Politics in America.* Stanford, CA: Stanford University Press, 2006.

Lansford, Tom. *Democracy.* New York: Marshall Cavendish, 2008.

Norris, Pippa. *Democratic Phoenix: Reinventing Political Activism.* New York: Cambridge University Press, 2002.

Pankhurst, Sylvia. *The Suffragette: The History of the Women's Militant Suffrage Movement.* 1911. Reprint, Mineola, NY: Dover, 2015.

Zakaria, Fareed. *The Future of Freedom: Illiberal Democracy at Home and Abroad.* New York: W. W. Norton, 2003.

Online

Global Voices. https://globalvoices.org/.

National Voting Rights Museum and Institute. http://nvrmi.com/.

Public Broadcasting Service. "Frontline: Voting Rights." http://www.pbs.org/wgbh/pages/frontline/voting-rights/.

United Kingdom Electoral Commission. "About My Vote." http://www.aboutmyvote.co.uk/.

SERIES GLOSSARY

accountability: making elected officials and government workers answerable to the public for their actions, and holding them responsible for mistakes or crimes.

amnesty: a formal reprieve or pardon for people accused or convicted of committing crimes.

anarchist: a person who believes that government should be abolished because it enslaves or otherwise represses people.

assimilation: the process through which immigrants adopt the cultural, political, and social beliefs of a new nation.

autocracy: a system of government in which a small circle of elites holds most, if not all, political power.

belief: an acceptance of a statement or idea concerning a religion or faith.

citizenship: formal recognition that an individual is a member of a political community.

civil law: statutes and rules that govern private rights and responsibilities and regulate noncriminal disputes over issues such as property or contracts.

civil rights: government-protected liberties afforded to all people in democratic countries.

civil servants: people who work for the government, not including elected officials or members of the military.

corruption: illegal or unethical behavior on the part of officials who abuse their position.

democracy: A government in which the people hold all or most political power and express their preferences on issues through regular voting and elections.

deportation: the legal process whereby undocumented immigrants or those who have violated residency laws are forced to leave their new country.

dual citizenship: being a full citizen of two or more countries.

election: the process of selecting people to serve in public office through voting.

expatriate: someone who resides in a country other than his or her nation of birth.

feminism: the belief in social, economic, and political equality for women.

gender rights: providing access to equal rights for all members of a society regardless of their gender.

glass ceiling: obstacles that prevent the advancement of disadvantaged groups from obtaining senior positions of authority in business, government, and education.

globalization: a trend toward increased interconnectedness between nations and cultures across the world; globalization impacts the spheres of politics, economics, culture, and mass media.

guest workers: citizens of one country who have been granted permission to temporarily work in another nation.

SERIES GLOSSARY

homogenous: a region or nation where most people have the same ethnicity, language, religion, customs, and traditions.

human rights: rights that everyone has, regardless of birthplace or citizenship.

incumbent: an official who currently holds office.

industrialization: the transformation of social life resulting from the technological and economic developments involving factories.

jurisdiction: the official authority to administer justice through activities such as investigations, arrests, and obtaining testimony.

minority: a group that is different—ethnically, racially, culturally, or in terms of religion—within a larger society.

national security: the combined efforts of a country to protect its citizens and interests from harm.

naturalization: the legal process by which a resident noncitizen becomes a citizen of a country.

nongovernmental organization (NGO): a private, nonprofit group that provides services or attempts to influence governments and international organizations.

oligarchy: a country in which political power is held by a small, powerful, but unelected group of leaders.

partisanship: a strong bias or prejudice toward one set of beliefs that often results in an unwillingness to compromise or accept alternative points of view.

refugees: people who are kicked out of their country or forced to flee to another country because they are not welcome or fear for their lives.

right-to-work laws: laws in the United States that forbid making union membership a condition for employment.

secular state: governments that are not officially influenced by religion in making decisions.

sexism: system of beliefs, or ideology, that asserts the inferiority of one sex and justifies discrimination based on gender.

socialist: describes a political system in which major businesses or industries are owned or regulated by the community instead of by individuals or privately owned companies.

socioeconomic status: the position of a person within society, based on the combination of their income, wealth, education, family background, and social standing.

sovereignty: supreme authority over people and geographic space. National governments have sovereignty over their citizens and territory.

theocracy: a system of government in which all major decisions are made under the guidance of religious leaders' interpretation of divine authority.

treason: the betrayal of one's country.

tyranny: rule by a small group or single person.

veto: the ability to reject a law or other measure enacted by a legislature.

wage gap: the disparity in earnings between men and women for their work.

INDEX

A

absentee ballots, 48, 50, 52–53
access, challenges to, 50–51, 52–53
Afghanistan, 50
African Americans, 35, 42, 44
African National Congress, 50
age for voting, 43
American Revolution, 42
apathy, 19, 26, 28, 34, 54, 56
Argentina, 44, 56
Australia, 12, 45, 54, 56
Australian Labour Party, 25
Austria, 45, 46

B

ballots, 31, 33, 41, 48, 50, 52–53
banning orders, 21
Belgium, 45, 56
bicameral, 29, 33
boroughs, pocket and rotten, 41
Brazil, 44
Brown, Michael, 14
Bulgaria, 46
Bush, George W., 36

C

California, 44
campaigns, political, 14, 26
Canada, 16, 46, 53–54
candidates, 31, 35
cantons, 29, 33
Catholics, 43
challenges to political participation, 19–28
  apathy, 26, 28
  defined, 19–20
  formal, 21, 23
  informal, 23, 25–26
Civic Welfare Training Service (CWTS), 12
Civil Rights Act of 1871, 44
Colorado, 33
Columbia, 50
Communist Party of Germany, 21, 23
compulsory voting, 56
conflict, 20
constituents, 16, 33, 37
constitutions, 33
consultations, political, 14, 16–18
contributions, 26
conventions, constitutional, 17–18
convicts, 46–47
Croatia, 31

cultural ideas, 25
CWTS (Civic Welfare Training Service), 12

D

Delaware, 42
demagogues, 39, 42
democracies
  characteristics of, 10
  defined, 9–10
  direct, 31–33, 35–38
  emerging, 48, 50
  representative, 33–34, 35–38
  suffrage and, 42
  threats to, 23
  voting in, 39, 41, 45–47, 48, 50
demonstrations, 14, 15, 17, 20, 21, 23
Denmark, 45
direct democracy, 31–33, 35–38
disadvantaged populations, 41
disenfranchisement, 44
donations, 14

E

early voting, 53, 54
Economist, The, 26
education, 12
Egypt, 50

INDEX

elections, 10, 14, 29–38
  defined, 29, 31
  direct democracy and, 29, 31, 33
  problems of, 35–38
  representative democracy and, 33–34
  winners in, 35
electoral colleges, 36
emergency responders, 12
emerging democracies, 48, 50
environment, 12
equality, 10, 15
Estonia, 45, 53–54
ethnicities, 16, 21, 23, 25, 42, 44
European Convention on Human Rights, 21
European Union, 31, 45
executive sessions, 21

F

Facebook, 17
feedback, 16
Ferguson, Missouri, 14
Fifteenth Amendment, 42, 44
Finland, 42, 46, 54
First Amendment of the U.S. Constitution, 21
focus groups, 16
formal political participation, 10–12
France, 43, 45, 46
franchise, 41
fraud, 51, 54, 56
French Socialist Party, 25

G

Germany, 23
Gore, Al, 36
governments
  dissatisfaction with, 14
  participation in, 10–11, 20, 21
  referendums and, 31
  services from, 12
"grandfather clause," 44
Great Britain, 41
Greece, 56

H

hackers, 53
hatred, 21
Hungary, 46

I

Iceland, 14, 42
identification (ID), 51, 53
income inequality, 15
India, 17
individuals, 12, 14
inequalities, 15, 23, 24
informal political participation, 10, 12–14
informed choices, 35
interest groups, 9, 14
Internet, 53
intimidation, 44
Ireland, 41
Italian Democratic Party, 25
Italy, 33

I-voting, 53

J

Jews, 43
Jim Crow era, 39, 42, 44
jury service, 12

K

Ku Klux Klan (KKK), 44

L

landowners, 41
laws, 51
Lebanon, 56
legislatures, 25, 33, 36
listening sessions, 16
literacy, 12, 44
Literacy Training Service (LTS), 12
Luxembourg, 45, 47

M

majorities, 34, 36
Malta, 46
malware, 48, 53
Maryland, 44
mathematics, 12
media, social, 17
military coup, 48, 50
military service, 12
minorities, 23, 25, 34, 35, 41, 42
movements, 15

N

National Democratic Party of Germany (NPD), 23

POLITICAL PARTICIPATION AND VOTING RIGHTS

national service, 9, 12
neo-Nazis, 19, 21, 23
Netherlands, the, 45, 47
New York, 15
New Zealand, 33, 42
99 percent, 15
noncitizens, 45
nonparticipation, 25
Norway, 16, 46

O
Occupy Wall Street, 15
officials, elected, 34
Oklahoma, 44
Old Sarum, 41
opinions, 10, 14, 21, 34, 35
organizations, political, 21, 23
organizers, 17

P
Parliament, 41
parties, political, 35
partisanship, 19
Philippines, 12
pocket boroughs, 41
policies, 10, 14, 16–18
political participation, 9–18
    consultations, 14, 16–18
    defined, 9–10
    formal, 10–12
    informal, 12, 14
    see also challenges to political participation
poll tax, 39, 44

poor, the, 41, 42
Portugal, 45
power, political, 11
process, political, 10, 20
property requirements, 42
proportional systems, 35
protests, 14, 15, 17, 20, 21
public opinion, 10, 14, 34, 35

Q
Quakers, 43
quotas, 25

R
race, 16, 20, 44
recalls, 33–34
Reconstruction, 44
redistribution, 42
referendums, 29, 31–32
registration, 14, 44, 54
religious restrictions, 42
representative democracy, 33–34, 35–38
Reserve Officers' Training Corps (ROTC), 12
rights
    of assembly, 21
    political, 35
    voting, 11
rotten boroughs, 41

Russia, 50
Rwanda, 25

S
Saudi Arabia, 50
Scotland, 17–18, 31, 44
Secure Electronic Registration and Voting Experiment (SERVE), 54
Singapore, 56
Slovakia, 47
social activities, 12
Socialist Reich Party, 21, 23
social media, 17
socioeconomic status, 19, 20
South Africa, 50
sovereignty, 29, 31
Spain, 46
students, 12
suffrage, 39, 41, 42–43, 45, 48, 50
Sweden, 25, 42, 45
Swiss People's Party, 32
Switzerland, 32, 33

T
taxes, 34, 39, 44
teaching, 12
tenants, 41
terrorism, 9, 14
Thailand, 54
town hall meetings, 17
Turkey, 50

INDEX

turnout, voter, 25, 26, 32
Twenty-Fourth Amendment of 1964, 44
Twitter, 17
tyranny, 9–10
tyranny of the majority, 29, 34

U

underclass, 42
United Kingdom
  jury service in, 12
  protests in, 21
  and Scotland, 18
  suffrage in, 41
  voting in, 25, 26, 42–43, 45–46
United States
  absentee ballots, 52
  electoral college in, 36
  executive sessions in, 21
  ID laws in, 51
  military service, 12
  minorities in, 35, 42
  protest movements in, 15
  referendums and, 33
  town hall meetings in, 17
  voting in, 41, 43, 45–46, 48, 54
universal suffrage, 42–43, 45, 48, 50
U.S. Constitution, 21, 44
U.S. House of Representatives, 25

V

violence, 14, 20, 21
volunteers, 14, 25, 26
voter ID laws (ID), 51
voting
  age, 43
  apathy, 54, 56
  compulsory, 56
  in democracies, 31–33, 39, 41, 45–47, 48, 50
  districts, 41
  early, 53, 54
  fraud, 51, 54, 56
  in India, 10
  methods, 35, 36–37
  online, 53–54
  participation, 31–32
  paying for, 41
  property requirements for, 42
  for recalls, 33
  representative, 11
  restrictions on, 42, 44, 45, 50
  turnout for, 25, 26, 32
voting rights, 39–47
  defined, 39, 41
  restrictions on, 45–47
  and universal suffrage, 42–45

Voting Rights Act of 1965, 42, 44
voting rights challenges, 48–56
  access and, 50–53
  apathy and, 54, 56
  defined, 48, 50
  new approaches to, 53–54

W

Western Europe, 21, 45
West Germany, 21, 23
whites, 35, 44
Wiltshire, 41
winners in elections, 35
women, 24–25, 41, 42, 50

Y

youth rights movements, 39, 45
YouTube, 17

ABOUT THE AUTHOR

Tom Lansford is a Professor of Political Science, and a former academic dean, at the University of Southern Mississippi, Gulf Coast. He is a member of the governing board of the National Social Science Association and a state liaison for Mississippi for Project Vote Smart. His research interests include foreign and security policy, and the U.S. presidency. Dr. Lansford is the author, coauthor, editor or coeditor of more than 40 books, and the author of more than one hundred essays, book chapters, encyclopedic entries, and reviews. Recent sole-authored books include: *A Bitter Harvest: U.S. Foreign Policy and Afghanistan* (2003), the *Historical Dictionary of U.S. Diplomacy Since the Cold War* (2007) and *9/11 and the Wars in Afghanistan and Iraq: A Chronology and Reference Guide* (2011). His more recent edited collections include: *America's War on Terror* (2003; second edition 2009), *Judging Bush* (2009), and *The Obama Presidency: A Preliminary Assessment* (2012). Dr. Lansford has served as the editor of the annual *Political Handbook of the World* since 2012.

PHOTO CREDITS

Cover: Wikimedia Commons/Department of Defense; iStock/EdStock; iStock/gaborbasch
iStock.com: 10 EdStock; 15 Jen Grantham; 16 EdStock; 27 carterdayne; 30 themoog; 46 LenaKozlova; 49 penguenstok; 51 @laurent; 52 Stephen Krow; 55 EdStock
Library of Congress: 43 Peter Pettus
Wikimedia Commons: 6 Al Jazeera English; 11 Rizuan; 13 Defense Imagery; 20 petergray1989; 22 jo-marshall; 24 Helene C. Stikkel, Department of Defense; 32 Yerevantsi; 34; Shiraz Chakera; 37 Infrogmation; 40 VCU Libraries